Old Shetland
Guthrie Hutton

German aircraft appeared frequently over Shetland in the early months of the Second World War. Sometimes they just made observation runs, but unluckily for Shetland, the thirteenth such visit, on 24 January 1940, proved to be a bombing raid. It did little damage, but these youngsters helped to milk the propaganda by displaying bomb fragments and a boat's nameplate.

**Dedicated to Douglas Smith who died before his collection of pictures,
which form the basis of this book, appeared in print.**

© 2009 Guthrie Hutton
First Published in the United Kingdom, 2009
Stenlake Publishing Limited
54-58 Mill Square, Catrine, KA5 6RD
www.stenlake.co.uk

ISBN 9781840334555

Shetland is noted for its diminutive animals: sheep, ponies and collies like these two standing guard above Ronas Voe. The distinctive shape of Ronas Hill in the background and the contrast between its red granite rock and the varied greens of the vegetation is very special, but the dogs seem more interested in the camera.

Sailing has always been popular in Shetland with traditional boats like these or modern yachts taking part in regattas at various places around the islands.

Some Further Reading

Cluness, A. T. (Editor), *The Shetland Book*, 1967.
Donaldson, Gordon, *Northwards by Sea*, 1978.
Ferguson, David M., *Shipwrecks of Orkney, Shetland and Pentland Firth*, 1988.
Finnie, Mike, *Shetland: An Illustrated Architectural Guide*, 1990.
Gifford, John, *The Buildings of Scotland: Highlands and Islands*, 1992.
Hulme, Malcolm (Compiler and Editor), *Local News (Volume 1)*, 2003.
Livingstone, W. P., *Shetland and the Shetlanders*, 1947.
Manson, T. & J., *Guide to Shetland*, 1932.
Nicolson, James R., *Shetland (revised edition)*, 1979.
Ritchie, Anna, *Exploring Scotlands Heritage: Orkney and Shetland*, 1985.
Shaw, John, *Water Power in Scotland: 1550-1870*, 1984.
Tait, Charles, *The Shetland Guide Book*, 2003.

Acknowledgements

This book has been based, to a large extent, on a splendid collection of old postcards and photographs gathered by Douglas Smith. The pictures covered every aspect and corner of Shetland and were a pleasure to work with. I must also thank Douglas' wife Sheila and brother Brian for their help with information and access to research material. I am grateful too to Willie Smith for allowing me to use the pictures taken by C. J. Williamson on pages 23 (lower), 26 (lower) and 27 (lower). My thanks also go to Eric Eunson and Laurence Robertson for help with pictures and information.

Introduction

Shetland's position, miles from any large land mass, has long been a source of irritation to map makers, but to those wandering the northern seas in boats it has been a landmark and haven. People settled on the islands in the Stone Age and the story of human habitation since that time has been pieced together from evidence gathered at some of the most remarkable archaeological sites in northern Europe. Shetland is also where the best preserved example of those puzzling structures, the brochs, is located. Who the broch builders were or why they needed such massive defensive towers is not known with any certainty, but it is presumed they were intended as a refuge to protect their occupants from sea-borne raiders like the Vikings.

Although they arrived as invaders, the Vikings eventually settled and when Norway emerged as a unified country in the ninth century, the Orkney and Shetland Islands were drawn into it. An earldom covering both sets of islands was created to rule them on behalf of the king, but following an insurrection in 1194, Shetland came under direct rule from Norway. The Battle of Largs in 1263 weakened Norway's hold on its distant territories and through the fourteenth century its influence in northern Europe began to wane. It was diminished further when the Kalmar Union of 1397 united the thrones of Norway, Sweden and Denmark under a single, Danish, monarch.

The islands were perhaps less important to the Danes than the Norwegians and so, when the marriage of Princess Margaret of Denmark and James III of Scotland was arranged in 1468, the Orkney and Shetland Islands became part of the deal. The two island groups were pledged as security for the princess dowry and when the Danes failed to pay, the islands effectively became part of Scotland.

To begin with, life went on much as before for the islanders and for the best part of 100 years the only material change will have been a growing familiarity with Scottish ways and Scottish words. Then it happened. In 1564 Mary, Queen of Scots granted her half brother Robert Stewart the Earldom of Orkney and Shetland, a position that gave him what amounted to absolute power over the islanders and, for the next 50 years, he and his son Patrick exercised it with crude brutality. During this bleak period they and their friends enriched themselves at the islanders' expense, and replaced the old Norse ways with a feudal system that left the people dependent on the whims of overlords.

The Act of Union was broadly welcomed in the islands, but by the end of the eighteenth century Britain was at war with Napoleon and a new oppressor stalked the islands as the Royal Navy's press gangs searched for 'volunteers'. The Shetlander's skill at boat handling had made them prime targets for this particular form of forced labour. Some men died in naval service, but many thrived and the sea became a preferable way of life to the grind of working a croft to pay rent to a landlord. Crofting legislation in the late nineteenth century removed some of the inequities of a system that had prevailed since the dark days of Earl Robert.

While all this was going on fishermen from Holland had been gathering every year off Shetland to fish for herring. Their activities pointed the way to an industry that suddenly took off in the 1880s and lasted into the 1920s before dwindling stocks ended the bonanza.

Through all the changes, Shetlanders have never forgotten their Viking roots and celebrate these at festivals like Up-Helly-Aa. Those Scandinavian connections are also reflected in the offset cross on the flag, designed in 1969 to mark the 500th anniversary of the transfer to Scotland: the blue and white colours are Scottish. The flag is flown everywhere, proudly proclaiming a distinct Shetland identity that came to the fore very effectively when North Sea oil was discovered. The benefits are evident everywhere and, with fish farming, tourism and traditional crafts adding to the economic mix, the Auld Rock is rocking on.

Crofters grew cabbages and other vegetables in small stone enclosures called planticrubs to protect them from the ravages of weather and sheep.

With the *Earl of Zetland* standing off, some visitors arrive at North Haven, Fair Isle in the 1950s. The small boat used to ferry passengers between the steamer and the pier could be lifted out of the water by the crane at the pier's end when the sea got rough.

Situated about 24 miles south of Sumburgh Head and roughly halfway between Orkney and Shetland, there is an awful lot of often stormy sea surrounding Fair Isle. For those in passing ships it is a potential hazard, but for the many species of birds that pass it on their annual migrations Fair Isle must stand out as a welcome refuge. This is why ornithologist George Waterston bought the island in 1948 and established a bird observatory in the huts of a former Royal Navy station. They are seen here looking south with the dramatic semi-detached headland, Sheep Craig, behind. The island became the property of the National Trust for Scotland in 1954.

In the days of sail, islanders using their own boats rescued many people from ships wrecked on Fair Isle. In recognition of this the Board of Trade based a lifeboat on the island in 1878. The boat was replaced in 1911 by this one proudly displayed by its crew, clad in cork life jackets. Further recognition of the danger represented by the island to shipping came in 1892 and 1893 with the establishment of Fair Isle South and Fair Isle North lighthouses.

Fair Isle Haa, seen in the centre of this view, is the island's principal domestic building dating from the early 18th century. The roof is thought to have been built using timber salvaged from wrecked ships. The Haa is situated at the south end of the island where most of the population lives in scattered communities.

Fair Isle is noted for its intricate knitting patterns and Shetland as a whole is famous for fine wools and distinctive knitwear. The process inevitably starts with the sheep which wander about the islands in their thousands, although only about a quarter of these are the native breed. These hardy little animals live out on the open, common land known as scattald, existing on sparse vegetation and seaweed. The wool is very fine and sheds naturally, so in springtime the sheep are gathered together to be rooed, a process where the fleece is plucked from rather than shorn from the sheep. As the picture shows this could be a communal activity.

It seems that almost every stage of the knitwear process could have a communal element to it as is evident from this picture of women carding the raw wool after it had been cleaned. To do this the wool is drawn between two flat, toothed implements to disentangle and align the fibres ready for spinning. The picture is also a fascinating record of a cottage interior.

This group of women is shown spinning the carded wool and knitting it into finished products. Behind them is a display of items, presumably made by them and other women for P. T. Robertson who used this picture to promote their Shetland Hosiery business. The intricate patterns of the knitwear were created using a variety of natural wool colours, the most common of which was a creamy white which could also be dyed, a skill said to have been taught to the knitters on Fair Isle by sailors from a ship of the Spanish Armada that was wrecked in 1588. The other natural colours included black, in reality a dark brown, a lighter brown known as moorit, and shaela, a greyish brown. These could also be blended together to create other shades.

Of all the wonderful articles made by Shetland's knitters, perhaps the most splendid are the gossamer thin shawls, so fine they could be drawn through a wedding ring. The wool for this lace knitwear did not just come from pure Shetland sheep, but was taken from the neck where the fleece was at its finest. This trio of knitters is proudly displaying a magnificent shawl that was, according to a note on the back of the picture, five foot six inches square and weighed only one and an eighth ounces.

Sumburgh, seen here looking west to Scatness and Fitful Head, had been a place of habitation for thousands of years before Robert Stewart, who became Earl of Orkney and Shetland in 1564, built a mansion house there. The Stewarts, or the Bruce family who subsequently took over the estate, erected other buildings on or near the site. In the foreground is the farmhouse and beyond that Sumburgh House built to the designs of architect David Rhind in 1866/67. It has since become a hotel and been extended more than once. Beyond it, on the shore of the voe, are the remains of Robert Stewart's first house that was given the name *Jarlshof* by Sir Walter Scott in his novel *The Pirate*.

When Scott saw *Jarlshof* it was half-buried in sand and he would have been unaware of the extraordinary multi-layered archaeological site that lay beneath it. Revealed by storms later in the nineteenth century, *Jarlshof*, or Sumburgh as it would have been known to earlier generations, included dwelling sites from the Stone Age to Viking times crowded onto the same site with a Pictish broch and topped by the sixteenth and seventeenth century houses built by the Stewart Earls. Another broch and Iron Age settlement site have also been revealed nearby at Scatness.

Clearly a significant place for many hundreds of years, Sumburgh has grown in importance for the whole of Shetland since the landing of the first plane here in 1933. At that time Sumburgh was no more than a flat grassy field, but within three years it was playing host to regular commercial flights from the Scottish mainland although, as the upper picture shows, the facilities remained quite rudimentary. The runway was hard surfaced during the Second World War, and after the war the nationalised British European Airways (BEA) took over from the early, small commercial operating companies. BEA used aircraft like this Dakota and later the ubiquitous Vickers Viscount for which the runways had to be extended. The discovery of oil off Shetland has resulted in massive expansion at Sumburgh and the erection of the Wilsness Terminal buildings in 1979.

The large house in the left foreground of this picture of Scholland was demolished to clear the line of the extended runway. Behind the house is the early school and behind that the village of Toab.

Scholland and Toab are part of the larger "toonship" of Virkie that also includes Exnaboe. It sits on rising ground to the north of the Pool of Virkie and, while these houses appear to have changed little, their occupants have had a grandstand view of the massive changes that have taken place at Sumburgh Airport.

Quendale, seen here looking south to a distant Sumburgh Head, was uncomfortably close to the main news story of January 1993 when the oil tanker *Braer* ran aground on Garths Ness, just off to the right of the picture. The ship had lost power in a storm and drifted onto the shore sparking fears of an environmental catastrophe. On this occasion, however, Shetland's wild weather proved to be its ally as gales dispersed the escaping oil. Out of the eye of the media storm Quendale's main attraction is the restored water mill seen in the centre of the picture.

The Quendale Mill, with its vertically mounted overshot wheel, is unusual in Shetland. It was built in 1867 and would have milled grain grown over a large area. In almost every respect therefore it differs from the distinctive little mills that were once so common throughout the islands that 500 or more are thought to have existed. These mills were worked with a horizontally mounted wheel, or tirl, a system believed to have been in use since Viking times and, although there is little evidence to support such a connection, they are sometimes known as Norse mills. These horizontal mills were built singly or in groups of two, three or more where the watercourse suited such an arrangement. Such mills, which served the needs of small communities, fell out favour around the turn of the nineteenth and twentieth centuries. The one shown here was photographed at Cunningsburgh, where the burns running swiftly off the hills to the west were ideal for driving the tirls.

The crofting township of Scousburgh is seen in the foreground of this view looking across the narrow strip of land that separates Muckle Sound on the right from the Loch of Spiggie, left. Formerly known as the Loch of Lunabister, Spiggie was a noted fresh water fishing loch, although in these more environmentally sensitive times it has become better known for its bird life and the wetland plants that thrive between it and the smaller Loch Brow, or Brew, to the south.

From 1896, visitors to the area could find accommodation at Spiggie Hotel, on the right of this picture, just a couple of minutes walk from the lochs. In the 1930s it was known as Spiggie House and owned by Mrs Flaws. Her advertisements offered first class accommodation on moderate terms. They also emphasised the good fishing and proximity to the lochs and Sandy Bay that made the location ideal for bathing and for children. The building has reverted to being known as a hotel and its appearance somewhat altered from the way it looks in this picture.

The Danish schooner *Martin Nisson* must have encountered some dreadful conditions on her passage to Stornoway with a cargo of timber. She had been at sea for nearly seven weeks when, in late December 1929, she came ashore near Scousburgh in a derelict condition. Her crew was missing.

With St. Ninian's Isle in close proximity it was perhaps inevitable that the church seen in this view of Bigton would be named after the saint. The church itself was built in 1905, while on St. Ninian's Isle, which is connected to the mainland by a beautiful sandy tombolo, is a much older church site with the remains of a twelth century building overlaid on an earlier chapel. An archaeological excavation here in 1958 unearthed a spectacular hoard of silver artefacts which became the subject of a bitter ownership dispute. This resulted in them being declared treasure trove and, to the dismay of Shetlanders, being lodged in the National Museum of Antiquities in Edinburgh.

In this view of Levenwick, on the east side of the mainland, a number of herring drifters can be seen in the distance riding at anchor in the bay. Its sheltered waters provided a safe haven over the years for a variety of seafarers from smugglers to fishermen. The empty driving seat of the little car in the foreground suggests that it was the photographer's own car and that he carefully positioned it to add interest to the foreground. Good photographers often did this and Jack (J.D.) Rattar of Lerwick was good.

Jack Rattar also knew a bad picture when he saw one, writing a note on the back of this one. It reads: "Nothing strange here but a walrus. I cannot catch it ashore, and a photo like this cannot show the size of it. Then it shifts about so, sometimes at Whalsay, then North of Bressay, then Cunningsburgh. This was taken at the Green Head. I have had many runs after it, but this is all I have got to show."

Hoswick, seen here in a picture from about 1900, is one of the many communities that make up Sandwick. The scene is still recognisable despite the addition of new housing.

At Cumliewick, on the opposite side of the bay from Hoswick, is Broonies Taing where a new pier, curing sheds and other facilities were built for the fishing industry and opened in August 1904 by Reginald MacLeod, Permanent Under Secretary for Scotland, who travelled to the ceremony from Lerwick on the steamer *St. Giles*. The facility had fallen into disuse by the1930s, but Broonies Taing got a new lease of life in the 1970s as an oil supply base.

Central Sandwick has grown substantially since this early twentieth century picture of the stores and bakehouse was taken.

The large house in the central background of this picture is Sand Lodge. The name is also used, as a single word, for the village that surrounds it. In the late eighteenth century Sandlodge became the location for copper mining, one of Shetland's more unusual industries. Welsh miners were brought to the area to open the mine, which worked two veins of ore, but was never active for very long at any one time. A concerted effort to work the mine started in 1872 and continued throughout that decade producing nearly 2000 tons of copper ore and 400 tons of iron ore in 1880. The mine closed the following year, reopened in 1920 and was finally abandoned two years later. Since its days as a mine Sandlodge has become known as the place to catch the ferry to and from the Island of Mousa, seen in the background of the picture.

The most complete and impressive broch is located on Mousa. These circular stone towers are unique to Scotland with the largest concentration in Caithness, Orkney and Shetland. They were defensive structures, erected mainly on coastal sites that could be cultivated or grazed, suggesting that their builders were farming people, fearful of a sea-borne aggressor. The Broch of Mousa is 50 feet in diameter at the base, 40 feet at the top and rises to over 40 feet in height.

Sandwick Church of Scotland was built in 1807 and its interior lined with timber a couple of years later. Seen here in an undated picture from the early twentieth century, it is decorated for harvest thanksgiving. Not only is there a fine display of crops and fruit, with even the paraffin lamps decorated, but significantly the walls have been draped with fishing nets indicating the importance to the community of the harvest from the sea.

Cunningsburgh, to the north of Sandwick, is an area of scattered crofting communities. One of these is Mail, seen here with a collection of fishermens' booths on the foreshore and the church and manse in the background.

The bridge and causeways linking the islands of East and West Burra at Bridge End are seen on the left of this view with the Baptist Church, which dates from 1904, on the extreme left of picture. The former Bridge End School, built on an islet at the head of South Voe, is on the right while the most prominent feature is the distinctive pink granite war memorial.

Hamnavoe was a small settlement of half a dozen houses at the start of the herring boom, but grew rapidly with rows of single storey cottages being built to create a fishing village more akin to Scotland than Shetland. The village thrived and declined along with the fishing industry and to help things along a new pier was built in 1956. Recent housing developments have been more random than the orderly rows of old giving Hamnavoe a more typically Shetland appearance.

Despite being close to the main centres of population the Burra Isles and the island of Trondra were cut off from them by the sea. Boats operated out of Scalloway as ferries, but as this picture shows getting supplies on and off could be a struggle.

The inconveniences of island life were consigned to history when the Trondra - Burra scheme was completed in 1971. The scheme consisted of two bridges, one linking West Burra with the Island of Trondra, and the other connecting Trondra to the mainland. Roads built between the bridges helped to transform island life and halt the then worrying decline in population. Trondra, which shelters Scalloway Harbour, is seen here at the narrow point where the bridge and connecting roads were built.

The view of Scalloway from the Scord is one of the most photographed in Shetland. It presents the town at its scenic best and encapsulates its major influences, the castle and the pier. Scalloway was Shetland's principal centre of population when Earl Patrick Stewart built his castle on the promontory between the bay and East Voe. It was from here that he exercised power and administered the law, but not for long because fifteen years after its completion in 1600 Earl Patrick was executed.

With its owner dead, the castle fell into disuse. Garrisoned briefly in the 1650s by Oliver Cromwell's soldiers, thereafter it slowly fell into disrepair. Traces of the colourful painted interior decoration, popular with Scottish nobility at the time of the castle's construction, were apparently still visible at the start of the eighteenth century. It is seen here about a hundred years ago and although ruined, still looks impressive behind the foreground carts loaded with cut peats.

The castle's decay was matched by a decline in Scalloway's fortunes, but things started to pick up through the early decades of the nineteenth century. The first Blacksness Pier was built in 1832 allowing trading vessels to come alongside. The boat in this picture is thought to be the schooner *Columbine* operated by Hay and Company between 1869 and 1914. The pier was extended into deeper water toward the end of the nineteenth century and it has been added to since, and with each pier extension the castle's commanding position on the promontory has been diminished.

Blacksness Pier was also used by fishermen and, as this picture of a boat with a whale on board shows, not just to land fish. Catching the unexpected was clearly an occupational hazard; a Sandwick boat arrived at Lerwick in 1936 with a section, five feet long, hacked from the tail of a creature that had become entangled in its nets. The men described it as about twenty feet long, as thick as a herring barrel, with two fins and a head like an eel or a sea serpent! Even allowing for exaggeration, it must have taken some skill to keep the boat afloat while dealing with such a terrifying incident, or while hoisting a whale aboard.

Fishing became an important industry for Scalloway in the 1820s when cod was the principal quarry. Herring was always a mainstay, but whelks and oysters also became a valuable harvest until overfishing ended that trade. By the end of the century the focus had shifted to the pursuit of haddock in the winter months and herring during the summer. In this picture herring are being cured and packed on Blacksness Pier against a backdrop of the castle and under the prow of an old sailing vessel drawn up on the shore of East Voe. Scalloway also became a centre of the kippering trade, which made for some spectacular fires when the kilns themselves went up in smoke.

A school was set up in Scalloway over fifty years before the building of the new Scalloway School in 1876. As the picture shows the site was at the junction of New Road and Castle Street, at that time on the edge of town and, while the long uphill trudge may have been daunting for some, there was plenty of space to play during breaks from lessons. The building was erected for the School Board, set up under the Education Act of 1872 which required every child between the ages of five and thirteen to attend school. Subsequent Acts have extended those early provisions and, while part of the old building remains in place, a much larger school has been erected alongside.

The part of old Scalloway between Castle Street and New Street, as traffic was funnelled in and out of Blacksness Pier, was a crowded place. This view from the castle, taken about 1910, gives a sense of how much was crammed in to a relatively small area. Many of the foreground buildings have since gone and the house in the centre, which is now used as a café and takeaway, has been rebuilt with a raised roof and peaked dormer windows instead of the square topped ones seen here.

Known locally as the Cong Church, the Congregational Church, at Braehead, was built in 1838. It was extensively reconstructed and redecorated in the first half of 1904, during which time the congregation worshipped at the Church of Scotland Parish Church. This picture was taken to mark the church's centenary in 1938.

The attractive, mainly nineteenth century cottages of New Street are now fronted by paving, hard landscaping and gardens, but with peat stacks on the shore and a Fifie fishing boat at the end of a jetty, the scene when this picture was taken was quite different. The picture is undated, but it was sent with a message that both asks and answers a question: "what do you think of old Scalloway from the New Street, I think on the whole it is very good." The sender also asks if the recipient knows any of the boys, but alas this time there is no answer.

There has been little change to the buildings on the right of this view along Main Street although the one in the foreground now houses the Scalloway Museum. On the left, the timber building with the round-topped upper window has been replaced with a two-storied modern structure that does little to enhance the townscape.

At the start of the twentieth century Scalloway had two hotels facing the bay, almost as many hotels as in Lerwick, although the latter did have more boarding houses. At that time James Reid was the proprietor of the Royal Hotel and Charles Lennie owned the smaller of the two, the Scalloway Hotel. It has since been extended while the Royal has become a Church of Scotland residential home and day care centre. The upper picture shows it early in the twentieth century while the lower multi-view postcard shows interior views from around the 1950s.

Prominent on the left of this view of Scalloway from the west are some of the 40 council houses, built to improve living conditions for local people. Construction began in 1938, but the following year, with the outbreak of the Second World War, fifteen of them were taken over to house forces personnel. The picture was probably taken after completion of the houses but before the war because there is a ship at the pier and the service to Scalloway and the west side of Shetland was discontinued in 1939. The ship appears to be the *St. Clair*, built in 1937 as the last steamer in the North Company's fleet. She was renamed *St. Magnus* in 1960 when a new ship named *St. Clair* was built.

The Royal Hotel is in the centre of this picture looking across the bay to the west. On the right is the Church of Scotland erected in 1840/41. This simple box-like structure appears in the picture to be harled all over, but the stone frontage has since been exposed, presenting an attractive contrast with the remainder of the building. In 2003 a memorial was unveiled on the sea front opposite the church to the men who had died in the Second World War operation known as the *Shetland Bus*. Much of the operation was based at the boatyard buildings on the left.

Overwhelmed by German forces, Norway capitulated in April 1940, but some people, including servicemen, escaped to Britain, making the hazardous North Sea crossing in small boats. Many landed in Shetland determined to carry the fight back to their homeland. A clandestine operation, which became known as the *Shetland Bus*, was organised with its headquarters at Kergord House and a base at Lunna. Some of the fishing boats that people had used for their escape sailed back to Norway carrying equipment and trained agents whose mission was to disrupt the Germans. The Lunna base lacked repair facilities and so in 1942 the operation moved to Scalloway where a slipway was built to maintain the boats. Norway's Crown Prince Olav visited the slip, which still bears his name, in October 1942. A plaque commemorating the event is on the right of this picture, with a group of women wrapped up against the weather.

The *Shetland Bus* operation was dangerous. Although the little fishing boats blended in to the Norwegian seascape they were vulnerable to bad weather and to enemy attack if suspected. Many were lost and with them many good men, so in 1943 the American Navy gave the operation three, fast, submarine chasers that were used for the rest of the war. *The Shetland Bus* contributed hugely to the war effort by tying down a large number of German troops and maintaining morale in occupied Norway. The story was told in a definitive book written by the operation commander, David Howarth, a British naval officer. He stayed on in Scalloway after the war and for a while ran the boatyard where the operation had been based. It is seen here in a picture from the late 1940s or early 1950s when the yard closed.

Much of this high ground, looking east from the vicinity of Ladysmith Road, to the west of Scalloway has been developed with new housing. The low bushy trees beyond the foreground houses are in what was the garden of the former Westshore mansion house. Above them in the distant background is the quarry on the Scord that has since grown into a substantial scar on the hillside.

The temporary looking huts of this herring station, at Port Arthur, on the west side of Scalloway Bay, give an insight into the seasonal nature of the industry, and the itinerant lives of the people who worked in it. The station had become disused by the end of the First World War although the abandoned shore facilities were later used for a variety of boat repair and servicing activities. Since 1992 Port Arthur has been the location of the North Atlantic Fisheries College.

The Shetland Ploughing Match Society held its annual competition at Berry Farm to the north of Scalloway on a dry, cold day in March 1904. Ten ploughs took part with two going head to head in the champion class. The winner was Andrew Halcro of Voe and because this was his third victory in a row, having also won in 1903 and 1902, he was able to keep the trophy. Mr. and Mrs. Robertson, whose field was used for the match, also provided refreshments and afterwards entertained the judges, committee and secretary to dinner.

Although there is some doubt as to their identity, this body of soldiers is thought to be the Scalloway platoon of the Home Guard. Often seen as figures of fun and immortalised as such in the television comedy *Dad's Army*, the Home Guard had to be prepared to meet any invasion and so men who volunteered for such a unit on Shetland would not have seen it as a joke. The islands were within easy reach of German occupied Norway and Home Guardsmen could have found themselves in the front line without the protection of internationally recognised conventions afforded to regular troops.

The early local photographers were keen to capture the islanders' way of life, perhaps realising that in a rapidly changing world scenes like this cottage interior would soon disappear. Jack Rattar, who took the picture, published it with the title, The But End.

Pictures of elderly people were also popular, perhaps to show that island life was long-lived, although the one on the left entitled *Old But Still Game* is almost more comic than illustrative of anything. The clothes are interesting, but the pictures also include some fascinating, if unintended details. The bottles in the window on the left suggest that it may have been a shop, while on the right the thatched roof is held down by a piece of drift wood weighted by a stone.

The role of women was important in a society like Shetland where the men could be absent from home for long periods of time, either at the fishing or serving on ships. In the upper picture women are seen on a beach, thought to be on Whalsay, burning seaweed to make kelp. Potash production from kelp flourished as an industry through the late eighteenth and early nineteenth centuries, but its use in the soap and glass industries was superseded and the process died. It enjoyed a brief revival in the late nineteenth century when, for a brief period, women burned seaweed in pits on the beach to produce kelp for use in the manufacture of chemicals.

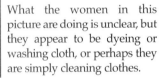

What the women in this picture are doing is unclear, but they appear to be dyeing or washing cloth, or perhaps they are simply cleaning clothes.

Although this picture has been staged for the camera, the woman and her little boy are carrying out the regular, tedious but important chore of shelling bait ready for the man of the household to use in line fishing.

Long before the home-grown herring boom started in the late nineteenth century, the rich grounds around Shetland had been exploited by Dutch fishermen. They realised the potential of Bressay Sound as a harbour and gathered there before the start of the herring season. Encouraged by their presence, local people gravitated to the area to set up booths and huts from which to buy, sell or barter goods with the fishermen. It was from this activity that Lerwick grew into a town. The Dutch continued to fish out of Lerwick well into the twentieth century as this picture of fishermen and boys shows.

Shetland's herring boom grew rapidly after 1880 with curing and packing stations being set up at places all around the islands. Early in the twentieth century the industry began to be concentrated at Lerwick. One of the main reasons for this shift was the building in 1907 of the new fish market, seen on the left of this picture. Boats were able to sell their catch at the market by auction rather than the earlier system of agreed prices. This led to increased returns, which attracted more boats, and the greater competition pushed prices even higher. Unusually for Shetland the market building was made of brick, but its foundations on made-up ground were unstable and it was demolished in the early 1950s.

The shoreline between North Ness and Garthspool became the location of numerous fishing stations, docks, boatyards and warehouses. The largest of these facilities was the Freefield yard developed by one of Lerwick's most successful merchants, Hay & Company and seen here in a picture from about 1900. The Hays built and repaired a variety of vessels at the yard and participated in the cod and herring fishing booms of the nineteenth and early twentieth centuries. Although disused by the latter end of the twentieth century the dock site has since become the location of the splendid Shetland Museum and Archives.

Steam drifters like the Lowestoft registered *Lord Howe*, seen here in a Lerwick slip dock, were a factor in the concentration of the industry at Lerwick. These boats were not subject to the vagaries of the weather and could get to the fishing grounds, or make port regardless of distance, whereas the extra miles could be crucial to a sail driven boat which could be thwarted by contrary winds while its catch deteriorated.

The fishing stations were busy places as this photograph by Jack Rattar shows. Women can be seen gutting fish at the box-like structures known as farlans. The word was used throughout the industry in Scotland, but is thought to have developed in Shetland from the foreland or foreshore where curing originally took place. Women of all ages appear to have been employed in this work as the two carrying a creel of fish in the centre of the foreground show.

The industry reached a peak in 1905 and then declined steadily. It lost some of its most valuable markets as a result of the First World War and although it picked up at times afterwards, it never regained its former prowess. When this picture of J. & M. Shearer's curing yard was taken in the 1950s annual landings were approximately the same as weekly landings had been at the peak and the curing industry was largely confined to Lerwick.

The herring boom brought many other ships to Lerwick. They arrived with cargoes like wood, coal, barrel staves and salt, commodities required either for the catching and curing the fish, or to keep the boats at sea. They left loaded with barrels of fish for markets on the European mainland or the British Isles. One such vessel, the *Scania*, which could be one of a number of Swedish ships that bore the name, is seen behind these three cheery women rolling a barrel along the pier.

The small freighter in this picture, the *Argyll*, is at the pier of one of Lerwick's many fish curers, A. Bremner & Company Ltd. When photographed she was loading barrels of herrings for Liverpool.

At the height of the herring boom a string of jetties jutted out from the shoreline at Holmsgarth. They were used by fishing stations to process fish for export in the ships waiting at anchor in the North Harbour. On land all this activity was serviced from a random clutter of sheds. After the boom years things quietened down for a while, but a series of changes transformed the area in the 1970s. It became the terminal for the new roll-on, roll-off ferry superseding Victoria Pier as the principal point of entry and departure for the islands. A new hotel was built and the oil industry created more development as a new boom hit Holmsgarth.

Despite the enormous scale of the herring boom and the level of activity it generated, the structures associated with it were generally insubstantial and often temporary as this Edwardian picture postcard of The Fisher Quarter shows. Sadly because of the card's poor print quality some detail has been lost, but it still conveys a strong image of a generally poor community. The houses, which in some cases appear to be little better than huts, were strung along the old North Road.

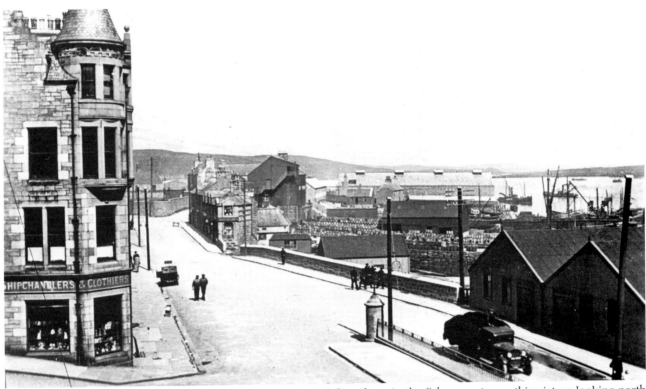

The structures closer to the town centre were more substantial than those in the fisher quarter, as this picture looking north from the junction of Commercial Road and Commercial Street shows. On the left, on the corner of Harbour Street, is Brentham Place, a substantial looking tenement building erected in 1900, architecture that would not have looked out of place in a city like Aberdeen or Glasgow. Opposite, on the site of the twin peaked corrugated iron building today is the Stewart Building with a single peaked roof. In the distance the fishing stations have gone, but the Malakoff works remain.

Shetland's strong maritime connections mean that organisations like the Missions to Seamen have received strong support over the years. This picture was taken at the Lerwick Institute in Charlotte Street on 11 September 1948. It was a Saturday, a flag day, and these happy volunteers were part of an effort throughout the islands that collected the handsome total of £168, a lot of money in those days.

Prior to the herring boom, cod was the Shetland fishermens' principal quarry, often sought in distant waters around the Faroe Islands, Iceland or Rockall. It was a hazardous occupation carried out in open or half-decked smack-rigged boats, but when the emphasis switched to herring, the men started to use fully decked Scottish boats known as Fifies. One of these is seen here in the late nineteenth century at a small jetty selling what appears to be cod directly to a small queue of local people. The ship in the background is thought to be a Norwegian barque known as *Walter*, which brought timber to the Lerwick boatyards and returned across the North Sea with fish.

This picture was given the title *Haddocks Alive* when it was published as a postcard about 1905. It shows a small boat alongside a slip adjacent to Victoria Pier and local people queuing to buy line-caught haddock. White fish, like haddock, became the mainstay of the fishing industry as the herring diminished.

The rapid rise in the herring boom brought equally rapid growth in Lerwick's prosperity and with it huge changes to the townscape. The Esplanade was created, filling the space in front of the old building line and, instead of lodberries and jetties jutting into the sea, a wharf wall was created, here occupied by a sailing vessel and a small steam launch. In the background are the turrets and gables of the Grand Hotel, a building that seemed to proclaim confidence in Lerwick's future prosperity.

Cars, buses and pedestrians jostle for space on the Esplanade in this picture taken during the inter-war years. At that time the herring industry was in decline, but boats still crowded the wharf along the Esplanade and filled the space between the fish market in the distance and Victoria Pier on the right. The pink granite drinking fountain in the centre foreground was erected in 1890 to mark the return of the Hull whaler *Diana* after an epic fourteen month long voyage in 1866/67, during which she was caught in the Arctic ice and lost thirteen crewmen, including nine Shetlanders.

The head of Victoria Pier was a popular gathering place for many people, including the Dutch fishermen seen here. Behind them are two contrasting early twentieth century buildings: in the centre, the Harbour Master's Office, built in 1906, is a fine example of the period's architecture. Beside it on the left is the less adventurous Victoria Building, erected in 1905. The picture shows the building being occupied by the Lerwick Co-operative Society. It was later used by the Aberdeen Savings Bank and ultimately Lloyds TSB who have since erected a modern building on the site.

The Victoria Building is on the right and the Harbour Master's Office on the left of this picture of Irvine Place looking toward Victoria Pier. The car in the foreground is sporting the PS letters given to all Shetland-owned motors under the first British vehicle registration system.

The Aberdeen, Leith, Clyde and Tay Shipping Company won a contract in 1838 to carry mail to Orkney and Shetland. It was the start of an association between the Aberdeen-based company and the islands that lasted for over 100 years. In 1875 the company name was changed to the North of Scotland & Orkney & Shetland Steam Navigation Company, a bit of a mouthful that was abbreviated in every day use to 'North Company'. As the service developed and the size of the ships increased, so did the shore facilities. Originally the lack of a suitable pier meant that the ships had to anchor off shore and people and goods had to be ferried to and from the land in small boats. All that changed in 1886 when the completion of Victoria Pier provided a deep-water berth adjacent to the town centre. The ships were part of island life and became familiar friends, and an essential link with the outside world, so their arrival or departure usually attracted a crowd of people. On this occasion the boat edging into the picture on the right is the *St Magnus*. She was built at Aberdeen in 1924 by Hall, Russell & Co. and was at the time the largest vessel in the North Company fleet.

A similar throng of people had gathered on Victoria Pier when this picture was taken in the 1930s with the second *St Sunniva* alongside.

As well as lifeline services to Orkney and Shetland, the North Company operated pleasure cruises to the Norwegian Fjords. After a successful first year of this venture in 1886 they ordered a new vessel, *St Sunniva*, from Hall, Russell & Company of Aberdeen. With the elegant lines and clipper bow of a luxury yacht she was a company favourite, not only cruising the Fjords, but occasionally also going to the Mediterranean on charter. Her cruising days were over by 1909 when she was put on the direct service between Aberdeen and Lerwick and she became a familiar sight at Victoria Pier. In April 1930 she ran aground on the Island of Mousa in dense fog. The passengers and crew were all saved, but the ship became a total loss.

The North Company's faintly bizarre reaction to the loss of this favourite ship was to order a similar vessel from Hall, Russell & Company of Aberdeen. Launched in 1931 the new *St Sunniva* looked magnificent, if a little unusual as a lifeline steamer while, as this picture shows, life on board could be like sailing on a mini ocean liner. She plied her regular summer run between Aberdeen and Lerwick throughout the 1930s, but during the Second World War was taken over by the Admiralty. Her speed made her ideal as a North Atlantic convoy rescue ship, but on the first trip her rigging became top heavy with ice, she turned turtle and sank with the loss of all hands.

As well as services to and from Scotland the North Company operated a ship, the *Earl of Zetland*, between Lerwick, Unst and all points in between. She is seen here at her usual berth on the north side of Victoria Pier and also on the left of the upper picture on the facing page. Built at Paisley in 1877, the Earl took over from a succession of sailing craft and small steamers that had operated the run for many years before her. Her original owner, the Shetland Islands Steam Navigation Company, was part owned by the North Company and then taken over by them in 1890.

The company replaced the ageing *Earl of Zetland* in 1939 with a new motor vessel of the same name, but she was no sooner on station than she was off again. With a number of ships being requisitioned by the Admiralty during the Second World War the North Company had to redeploy the remaining vessels. The new Earl went south to work the Pentland Firth crossing while the old Earl came out retirement and served the north islands for another six years. The second *Earl of Zetland* is seen here in the 1950s on the same berth at Victoria Pier used by her predecessor. She continued in service until 1975 when the introduction of vehicular ferries between the mainland, Yell and Unst made her redundant.

For as long as people have wanted to cross between Lerwick and the island of Bressay there have been boats to ferry them. The one in this picture was formerly a launch from the battle cruiser *Hindenburg*, one of the German warships scuttled at Scapa Flow in Orkney in 1919. She was acquired for use as the Bressay ferry in 1935 and continued to ply the route until 1975. She was used by the engineering firm Malakoff until the late 1990s and has since been donated to the Shetland Museum. She is seen here approaching her usual landing place, the slipway in the Small Boat Harbour adjacent to Victoria Pier. Although at first glance the ship in the background appears to be *St Sunniva* she was actually a private yacht .

Lerwick's famous Up-Helly-Aa celebrations grew out of earlier festivities to mark the end of mid-winter. Fire and guizing were always part of these older activities, but by the latter end of the nineteenth century they had become too boisterous for some folk and were curtailed. The happy compromise that evolved from this difficulty was the present festival which, in its early days, used the head of Victoria Pier as the burning place for the galley.

The proclamation for the Up-Helly-Aa festival is displayed at the Market Cross, seen through the gap in the buildings in the middle of this late 1950s picture. The distinctive Ellesmere Buildings, which date from 1906, are on the right while in the centre is one of Leask's buses waiting on its stance. To its left, the K Shoe sign painted on the gable has outlasted the Goodlad and Goodlad shop name that went with it. Anderson's Warehouse has become something of an institution in Lerwick as has The Lounge off Market Square where musicians gather on certain evenings to raise the rafters with a unique, drink-fuelled brand of local music. Great!

The Ellesmere Buildings and another Leask bus can also be seen in the central background of this picture. Although undated it appears to have been taken a year or two earlier than the upper view and looks across the Small Boat Harbour, created in 1913-15 by the building of a second pier to the south of Victoria Pier. On the left is the back of the post office building occupying a site between the waterfront and Commercial Street.

This late Victorian picture was taken before the Small Boat Harbour was created and was later used as a postcard with the title *A Northern Venice*, a description often used by publishers for the south end of Lerwick although the old tolbooth in the centre of the picture could hardly be regarded as a double for St. Mark's. The tolbooth was completed in 1770 and used as the islands' administrative centre until completion of the new County Buildings in 1876. The distinctive clock tower was removed in 1927, but has since been reinstated as part of the building's restoration. The buildings on the right have been removed to make way for the realignment of Church Road and the Esplanade.

The title *A Northern Venice* was also given to this picture when it was used as a postcard, and seen from this angle, with buildings rising straight out of the water, the description does seem appropriate. Behind the immediate waterfront buildings is the Queen's Hotel, which can also be seen in the upper picture. Built in the 1860s it also incorporated some older structures, one of which was used as a billiard room. It had a window from which, according to a message written in 1905, it was quite easy to drop right into the sea, presumably after losing a rash bet.

The buildings projecting into the water are known as lodberries. They evolved from the rocks or piers used to load and unload boats and were thus built as landing places. Boats could come alongside or in some instances go inside lodberries, a gate or doorway can be seen behind the building in the centre of the upper picture. Tunnels have been discovered connected to some lodberries, suggesting they were also handy places for smugglers to operate from. Prior to the development of Lerwick's piers and wharfs, the whole of the town's shoreline would have resembled the south end.

The photographer here has wisely chosen a calm day with the tide out to take this view of Commercial Street from the beach below the Knab. The scene has changed little although some of the old buildings have been replaced with modern flats. One that has survived is the large house on the left known as the Old Manse. Dating from the late seventeenth century, it is Lerwick's oldest house.

The upper of these two pictures shows Commercial Street looking from Craigie's Stane toward Water Lane where the old houses have been replaced with modern flats. To the south of Water Lane is Quendale House, a mid-nineteenth century laird's town house set back from the street line, from where the lower picture of a flying boat was taken. The arrival of machines like this in the early 1930s caused much excitement. One of the most significant was in August 1931 when the American pilot Parker Cramer and his Canadian mechanic L. D. Paquette diverted to Lerwick on a flight from Detroit to Copenhagen. They had encountered bad weather after leaving their last scheduled stop at the Faeroe Islands and landed at Slates Bay. Their machine drew crowds of interested onlookers as did their take off for Denmark, but they never made it and a few weeks later the crew of a trawler found wreckage from their plane. Undeterred by the tragedy, the Trans-American Airlines Corporation proposed a service from Detroit to a number of European destinations, including London via Lerwick, but nothing came of it. Flying boats were used heavily during the Second World War prompting the development of new machines, one of which was known as the *Shetland*. Two prototypes were built, but it never went into production for either military of civil use.

Commercial Street is Lerwick's principal shopping street, as is evident from this early 1950s picture looking south from Market Square. In the centre of the picture the street widens to form another small square with on one side the Royal Bank of Scotland building, which dates from 1871, and on the other side the post office: the public telephone box marks its location. The post office had previously been located in the old Union Bank building and then from 1878 in the Tolbooth, before moving to the new building, erected to the designs of architect W. T. Oldrieve in 1910.

In the days when all of Shetland's communications with the outside world came and went by sea, it made sense for the post office to be in close proximity to Victoria Pier. As well as everyday items, the mail boats brought the promise of news from home, and there were many people working in Shetland anxious for that. This picture is said to show Dutch fishermen congregating outside the post office waiting for the mail brought by the overnight boat to be distributed.

The lower right of these three pictures was used as a postcard with a message that is a fair description of Commercial Street. It reads: "the main street is paved from edge to edge with no pavements … people just stand in the middle and talk and when the one bus an hour passes they just plaster themselves against the wall to let it pass." While to that visitor the street seemed confined, some parts were once even narrower and more congested, as the upper picture shows. Entitled *The Roost* it dates from the nineteenth century while the lower pictures, from the first half of the twentieth century, show much the same section of street and the changes that had taken place over the years. One of the most obvious differences is the Grand Hotel built to the designs of architect William Hamilton Beattie in 1887, a date which helps to determine the age of the upper picture. With its imposing stair and decorative plasterwork, the hotel offered upmarket accommodation for steamer passengers. The frontage of the Union Bank building is in the foreground of the lower left picture.

The Union Bank building in the upper left of these three pictures was designed by the architect John J. Burnet and built to replace an earlier building, destroyed by fire in 1903. The foundation stone was laid at the end of August 1904 and the new bank was completed in 1906. The Union was a Glasgow-based bank that grew by acquiring a number of small local banking companies, until it was itself taken over by the Bank of Scotland in 1954. The upper right picture, taken about 1910, shows a shop with an ornamental frontage that was designed and built ten years earlier by John M. Aitken. A physical connection has since been made between it and the adjacent building. In the lower picture clog shod Dutchmen clatter along the street. The Shetland Hosiery shop on the left offered quality hand-made knitted goods at moderate prices including fine lace shawls, scarves, gloves and light, warm underclothing. Across the street, stationer William K. Conochie stocked a large range of novels and holiday reading as well as gramophones, wireless sets and fishing tackle.

Lerwick was originally sandwiched between the shoreline on one side and steeply rising ground on the other. Over time, the building up of the Esplanade created more space between sea and street, while on the landward side the town expanded up the hill along narrow lanes and closes. Entering or leaving Commercial Street through gaps in the buildings, or with entries spanned by buildings, these lanes were originally named after the people who owned or developed them, but were renamed in the mid nineteenth century. The upper left picture shows Gardie Court, formerly Gilbertson's Court. Law Lane, previously Sheriff's Closs, is on the upper right and the lower picture shows some now demolished houses in Mounthoolie Street.

The upper of these three pictures shows the former Tait's Closs, now Reform Lane, while the lower pictures show Hangcliffe Lane. Its earlier name, Steep Closs, is the title the photographer gave to the picture on the left, suggesting that the old names remained in common usage for some time after they were changed. Much of Lerwick's population lived in these lanes, but when the new town expanded across the high ground, well-to-do people moved out and the lanes degenerated into slums. Faced with this problem in the early 1970s the local authority, in common with councils throughout Scotland at the time, responded by clearing away many of the old buildings. In the process old Lerwick lost much of its character.

Some of the close entries can be seen in this picture looking south along Commercial Street with the Grand Hotel in the centre of the background. The name of Pilot Lane can be seen above the handcart, and Burns Lane is between the Soda Fountain and Ice Cream signs on the right. The very narrow Nicholson's Closs runs down towards the Esplanade between the buildings on the left. The picture is undated but, judging from the clothes people are wearing, it appears to have been taken in the 1920s or 1930s.

Although the shop signs on either side of Burns Lane have changed, the entry can be seen in this 1950s view looking north toward Charlotte Place. On the right is the building occupied then as now by the Clydesdale Bank. It was designed and built in 1892 by John M. Aitken who erected many of Lerwick's finest buildings. From the evidence of this structure and the shop on page 51 he appears to have enjoyed embellishing his designs with turrets and crow-stepped gables.

At the northern end of Commercial Street is Charlotte Place, seen here in a picture from 1937. Lipton's shop on the right, now occupied by Boots the Chemist, is in the former Royal Hotel building. Lipton's was one of a chain of grocery shops started by Sir Thomas Lipton in the Anderston area of Glasgow in 1871. He rose from very humble beginnings to amass a considerable fortune, much of which was spent in a dogged and ultimately unsuccessful pursuit of sailing's most glamorous prize, the Americas Cup.

James S. Smith sold butcher meat, fruit and vegetables for many years from this shop. It can also be seen at the corner of the large tenement in the background of the lower picture on the facing page. James MacPherson, one of Lerwick's early photographers, also conducted business at this end of Commercial Street, but in 1875 his studio was destroyed by fire. At the time there was no fire brigade, only fire-fighting equipment. It was deployed by the superintendent of police who managed to get the blaze under control, but not before the studio and a lodberry underneath it were destroyed. An adjacent building used by the tax authorities was also damaged.

The idea of building a fort at Lerwick emerged during Oliver Cromwell's war with the Dutch, but was dropped when the war ended in 1654. King Charles II was on the throne when the Second Dutch War broke out the following decade and this time a fort was built, but was abandoned and largely dismantled as part of the peace treaty. Another decade, another war and in 1673 Dutch sailors overwhelmed the fort, burning it and much of Lerwick. For over 100 years thereafter the failed fort remained a ruin, but in 1781, with France making mischief, it was rebuilt and a barrack block erected. The renewed facility was named Fort Charlotte after the Queen.

Lerwick was buzzing on the back of the herring boom and the town had begun to spread onto the high ground beyond the crowded slum-like lanes when the work on the town hall began. It was built in 1884 to the designs of Inverness architect Alexander Ross although, instead of rising to the point of a graceful central spire as he proposed, it was topped with a dumpy tower on the suggestion of the contractor, John M. Aitken. While architects ponder the merits of that change, local argument centres on whether, with its back to the harbour, the hall was built facing the wrong way. Right or wrong, the alignment of the town hall provided a good setting, 40 years later, for the war memorial set between Upper and Lower Hillhead.

When it became clear that the bodies of men killed during the First World War would not be brought home for burial, the people of Shetland, in common with those throughout Britain, sought to mark the sacrifice in a communal way. The memorial, a simple granite cross, designed by the Edinburgh architect Robert Lorimer, was unveiled on 6 January 1924 by Mrs Thomas Hardy of Girlsta who had lost three sons in the conflict. Her personal tragedy was echoed in the high losses sustained by Shetland as a whole, with 630 names recorded on the eight bronze tablets around the base of the memorial. Additional wings, with plaques listing the names of those who had died, were added to the memorial after the Second World War. A very high proportion of the men had been in the Merchant Navy.

St Ringan's United Presbyterian Church, seen here and in the background of the upper picture, was erected at Lower Hillhead in 1886. It became a part of the United Free Church after the amalgamation of the Free and United Presbyterian Churches in 1900, and a church of the Church of Scotland following its union with the Free Church in 1923. No longer used for worship it has been converted for use as the public library with an attractive space for local studies on a mezzanine floor next to the circular stained glass window in the north gable.

The town hall was a splendid facility, used for a wide range of activities one of which was the annual production by the Lerwick Musical Society, an event that was eagerly anticipated in the town. In March 1926 the Society staged Gilbert and Sullivan's *Patience* and the picture is thought to show Mrs. T. Marshall who starred in the title role, the first time she had taken a leading part.

Dancing was also popular at the town hall, although this picture obviously shows something more than a mere Saturday night hop. The formal clothes, the evidently fancy movements and footwork and the number on the back of the male dancer on the right, suggest that this was a competition, probably between Shetland and Orkney. Such events were eagerly anticipated and taken very seriously.

Inter island competition was also keenly contested on the sports field as it still is. In May 1934 the womens' hockey teams from Orkney and Shetland lined up at Gilbertson Park for what turned out to be a classic. Orkney led at half time by a goal to nil, but sixteen minutes into the second half Miss E. Robertston levelled with a goal for Shetland. The score was still even at full time and an extra fifteen minutes were played, but the sides could not be separated and so, as the existing holders, Shetland was awarded the Lady Hamilton Cup. It is seen here being presented to Miss L. Andrews, the Shetland captain, by County Convenor Mr M. Shearer. On the same day Shetland's footballers trounced Orkney by four goals to nil.

Lerwick Football Club, formed in 1878, started out by playing rugby, but football took over to become the main sport for young Shetland men. The weather dictates that the game is usually played during the summer months with teams drawn mainly from Lerwick and Scalloway competing in a senior league for a number of trophies. This team was photographed at Gilbertson Park, named after Robert P. Gilbertson, the benefactor who gifted the park to the town in 1897.

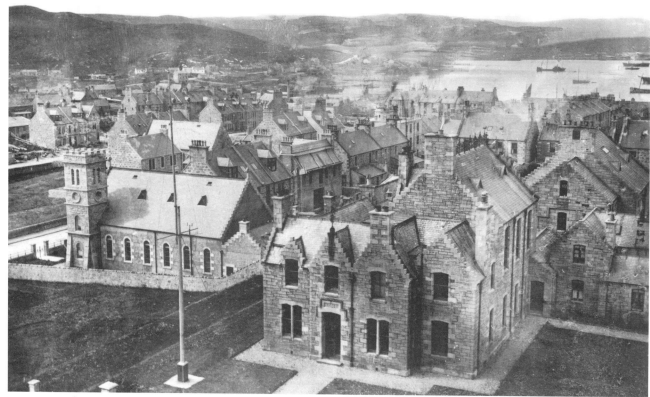

Views from the town hall tower were popular with photographers. This one looks across the County Buildings, built by local contractors to the designs of Edinburgh architect David Rhind. Fireproof rooms were incorporated into the structure to ensure the safety of official papers and the complex also included a two-storey prison block on the right of the picture. The Sheriff Clerk, county officials and prisoners from the old Tolbooth in Commercial Street completed their move to the new building in August 1876. To the left, the church-like building is St. Clement's Hall, built in 1911 as a hall for St Columba's Parish Church and a place of worship for Dutch fishermen.

This view from the town hall tower looks west to King Harald Street and its intersection with Union Street. To the left is the building erected in 1901/02 as the Central Public School by Lerwick's principal architect/builder of the time John M. Aitken. It has subsequently become the Islesburgh Community Centre. To the right is Islesburgh House, also constructed by John M. Aitken to the designs of architect Alexander Campbell. It was built in 1907 for Andrew Smith, one of the principal entrepreneurs involved in the herring boom, and has since become a youth hostel.

When the lanes that climb up from Commercial Street get to the top, the street that most of them join is the appropriately named Hillhead, seen here looking north. Law Lane's junction with the street is adjacent to the building on the right with the prominent gable, and further right, where some boys can be seen, is the top of Navy Lane. The Adam Clarke Methodist Church, erected in 1872, is on the left, partly obscured by a wall that has since been replaced by lock-up garages.

The oldest surviving church building in Lerwick is St. Columba's Parish Church in Greenfield Place. It was erected to the designs of Edinburgh architect James Milne and completed in 1829. A number of interior modifications, including the enlargement of the organ, which had been installed in the 1870s, were carried out just before this picture was taken in 1897.

Young Shetlanders going to secondary school had to do so in Lerwick. For many it was impossible to travel to and from home and so they had to find somewhere in the town to board. This problem was solved for girls with the building of the Bruce Hostel. Paid for by Robert Bruce of Sumburgh, work on it began in 1914 although it was not completed for occupancy until 1923. A similar facility for boys, the Janet Courtney Hostel, was completed in 1939.

In the centre of this picture, looking north from the Bruce Hostel, is St. Magnus Episcopal Church. It was built to the designs of architect Alexander Ellis and consecrated in August 1864 by Bishop Suther of Aberdeen. Alexander Ellis also designed the distinctive tower, added in 1891. Modern housing has since obscured this view.

Modern housing would, as with the picture on the facing page, make it impossible to replicate this view. Burgh Road is in the foreground and its intersection with Scalloway Road is on the right. Just above the chimneys of the house in the central foreground is the original Gilbert Bain Hospital. Its foundation stone was laid in 1901 and the building was completed the following year. A new Gilbert Bain Hospital was built sixty years later.

Sound was a crofting township. Its proximity to Lerwick meant that the crofters could provide milk and other provisions to the inhabitants of the larger town, but after the burgh boundary was extended in 1966 to include Sound, the crofts were replaced by housing.

The island of Bressay forms the east side of Lerwick Harbour. It is also a place where Lerwegians have traditionally gone for recreation. A short crossing on the ferry followed by a walk to the top of the Ward Hill was a favourite for those seeking spectacular views or going for a midsummer midnight picnic. These Edwardian ladies have gone in the opposite direction from the pier, north for about three-quarters of a mile to the standing stone at Keldabister.

The north end of the island was also a place of contrasts in building construction. The upper of these two pictures shows a structure shaped like a boat and roofed with one, not unlike the Scottish Parliament building in Edinburgh. It was photographed at Gunnista, close to Beosetter where the lower picture was taken in July 1936.

Much of Bressay, with the exception of the area around Gunnista, was depopulated in 1871 when John Walker, the factor acting for the landowner Miss Mouatt, evicted crofters to make way for sheep. The same happened on the small neighbouring Isle of Noss although instead of just sheep it was used to breed Shetland ponies for the Marquis of Londonderry's Durham coalmines. This picture looks from Bressay across Noss Sound to the smaller island.

A visit to the cliffs of Noss in a modern motor vessel is a relatively comfortable experience, but when this picture was taken people went out in small open boats to witness the sights and sounds. The boat here is being controlled with the oars while the sail has been tightly furled to ensure the craft is not swept off station by a rogue puff of wind. The importance of the Noss sea bird colonies was recognised in 1955 when the island was made into a national nature reserve.

Under Norse rule Shetland was divided into a number of districts which each held an assembly, known as a Vorting, to reaffirm laws and settle disputes. Some of these assemblies have left their mark on present day place names: Aithsting, Delting etc., although the most significant is Tingwall where the supreme court, the Alting, was held every summer the picture shows the wide Tingwall Valley where the assembly was held. All free men were expected to attend the Alting because it had superiority and could hear grievances arising from decisions taken by the lesser assemblies.

Whales were sometimes driven ashore by islanders, principally to make oil from the blubber. Traditionally the proceeds of such a cull were shared between the Earldom, the landowner on whose foreshore it took place and the men who carried it out, but in 1888 the inequity of this three way split was challenged by men from Hoswick. The Sheriff in Lerwick ruled in their favour and his decision was upheld in the Court of Session in Edinburgh, so from then on the men were more fairly rewarded although not for long, because by the early twentieth century, when this picture was taken at Weisdale Voe, the practice was already in decline.

The Bridge of Strom, seen in the upper of these two pictures, spans the narrow gap between Stromness Voe and the Loch of Strom. It has been upgraded since the start of the oil boom along with the rest of the road between Lerwick and the west. The road has also been realigned at Weisdale Bridge superseding the structure in the lower picture. Weisdale Kirk, beyond the bridge, was built as a Free Church in 1863.

During the middle decades of the nineteenth century a number of crofters from Upper Weisdale were evicted. Once the tenants had been cleared, the owner divided the land into large holdings and leased them to farmers. The new farms were given new names, one of which, Flemington, was subsequently changed to Kergord. It became one of the few places where trees grew on the islands, not just in the garden of the house as seen here, but also in a plantation created mainly in the second decade of the twentieth century.

The boats drawn up on the red sands of the splendid curving bay at Reawick indicate that this was once a thriving fishing community. The industry's importance had diminished by the time the picture was taken around the turn of the nineteenth and twentieth centuries. The complex of buildings on the shore contained shops and dwellings while Reawick House, on the slope behind it, was an old haa that was also used later, for a time, as a hotel.

Skeld was once a centre for the line-caught cod fishery that started the nineteenth century with only a few boats, but grew rapidly and peaked in the 1870s. At its height a variety of smack-rigged boats was engaged in this activity with some sailing to fishing grounds off the Faeroe Islands, Iceland and Rockall. The catch was salted on board and on arrival at Skeld and other ports was dried ready for export. Boats and men were sometimes lost in this dangerous and arduous work and this, coupled with competition from fishermen local to the distant grounds, led to the demise of this type of fishing.

These children were, according to a message on the picture, all dressed up for a Sunday school picnic in July 1914. They are either from or at Sand, a place with many religious associations. A Roman Catholic church here was used after the Reformation for Episcopal and then Presbyterian worship, before it was replaced about 1780 and again after the Disruption of 1843. Men from a wrecked ship of the Spanish Armada are also believed to have built a church on Kirk Holm, just off the shore.

These children, also thought to be from a Sunday school, were photographed at Walls beside the little burn that drains the Lochs of Kirkigarth and Bardister behind the village. In the background is Voe House, an eighteenth century double house with one half in the early stages of ruin.

Being the centre for a widely scattered community, Walls was well served with churches. There was St. Paul's Parish Church, beside the road to Walls Pier, the Congregational Church in the centre of the village and the Methodist Church, beside the road to and from Bridge of Walls. It is seen here with a Sunday evening congregation posing outside for a picture that is thought to date from the 1950s.

In the centre of the front row of the upper picture is a venerable gentleman sporting a drooping moustache. He looks very like the man in this picture, Robert Isbister, a Methodist lay preacher who was born in the early 1870s at Dale, where the picture may have been taken. He appears to have created his own little planticrub to protect his flowers from marauding animals.

Perhaps the most distinctive building at Walls is Bayhall a three-storied haa, seen here in an early twentieth century picture. The building was restored and converted into flats in the late 1970s.

Named after the numerous voes that indent the surrounding area, Walls, or Waas as it should perhaps more properly be spelled, sits at the head of Vaila Sound. Sheltered and protected by the island of Vaila the harbour was well placed for the herring and other fisheries through the nineteenth century although it declined in importance with the rise of Lerwick. The fishing station on the pier is seen here with the farlan in the background, behind another venerable gentleman and some fisher lassies rolling herring barrels into a stack. In the distance, in the top left hand corner of the picture is the Congregational Church. The pier is still used by the Foula ferry.

The distinctive shape of Foula, with its five hills, can be seen on a clear day from much of the mainland's west coast, but at its nearest point the island is thirteen and a half miles away. The weekly mail boat from Walls was, before the construction of an airstrip in the 1970s, the only contact with the outside world and even then the often turbulent sea ensured that no crossing could be guaranteed. At times Foula has been threatened with depopulation and it was used in 1936 as the location for *Edge of the World*, a feature film based on the enforced evacuation of the island of St. Kilda.

The island of Papa Stour is steeped in history. Its name, which means big island of the priests, was given to it by the Vikings when they found it occupied by an early Celtic monastic settlement. A sword dance of apparently Norse origin but performed by medieval European characters has survived as an intriguing folk custom. In the early nineteenth century the Earl of Balcarres effectively imprisoned his son, the Honourable Edwin Lindsay, on the island because he had refused to fight a duel. By the early 1970s the island's population had dropped below twenty, but an advertisement attracted young people from all over Britain seeking an escape from the rat race. Most of them found the conditions too rigorous, but some stayed on what became known for a while as *Hippy Isle*.

Sandness, on the mainland side of the Sound of Papa, is seen here looking east along the beach at Melby. It is a delightful spot overlooked by Melby House, out of the picture to the right. In the nineteenth century, while some landowners were clearing crofters off their land to make way for sheep, Mr. Scott, a naval surgeon who was the proprietor of the house, gained a favourable reputation by refusing to evict his tenants and treating them fairly.

During the First World War the Royal Navy based what it called the 10th Cruiser Squadron at Swarbacks Minn, an arm of St Magnus Bay. It included a number of so-called Armed Merchant Cruisers, ocean liners fitted with a six-inch calibre gun which, because they were fast, were used to patrol the waters to the north and west of Shetland to prevent German naval vessels breaking out into the North Atlantic. On the left of this picture is *Kildonan Castle*, a Union Castle Line ship once familiar in South African waters, but seen here with her beautiful lilac-grey hull stained by rust from neglect and a harsher environment. One of the squadron's ships, the White Star Liner *Oceanic*, achieved a kind of fame by running aground on a well-charted reef off Foula in fine weather, a victim of a confused command structure and dreadful navigation.

Voe, at the head of Olnafirth, is often said to resemble a Norwegian village, although the description really only fits Lower Voe seen here from the main north-south road. The scene has changed little over the years, although it has been altered by significant tree growth and an extended breakwater and marina. Voe was once the home of Thomas M. Adie and Sons, one of Shetland's best known businesses which traded in a variety of commodities from knitwear, tweed and tea to its own Adiesons brand of flour and oatmeal.

Olnafirth was the location of one of four whaling stations established by Norwegian companies, with the government's blessing, in 1903 and 1904. Two were at Ronas Voe and the other at Collafirth. They were not popular. The smell was awful, the mess dreadful and fishermen thought that whaling activities would lead to the demise of the herring industry. There were protests and demonstrations, but they failed to stop the industry that assumed some importance in the years leading up to the First World War.

With a small settlement at Ham on its west side and a few crofts like these spread along on the east side, Muckle Roe was as remote as any island, despite being separated from the mainland by only a narrow strip of water. All that changed in August 1905 when a new bridge, built across Roesound from the Ness of Busta to Muckle Roe was opened.

Roesound Bridge, seen here under construction, was financed mostly out of public funds, but a quarter of the money came from public subscription and much of that came from local people who gathered to witness Miss Inkster of Brae perform the opening ceremony. They then walked across the bridge to hear the Rev'd. Mr. Rogers, United Free Church minister of Brae, offer a dedicatory prayer. The bridge effectively made Muckle Roe part of the mainland and it has continued to provide a vital link for the islanders. It was widened and strengthened in 1947 and replaced by a new bridge in 1998/99.

The North of Scotland and Orkney and Shetland Shipping Company promoted Hillswick as a tourist destination. There was no pier and so the ship had to stand off while the passengers disembarked onto small boats that took them ashore to the jetty in the foreground of this picture. In Edwardian times the road would have been little better than a track, so this way of arriving at their destination must have made Hillswick seem very remote to people from the south.

The boats that ferried people to and from the steamers were known as 'flit boats' and one of these is seen here at Hillswick with the steamer in the background. It's a big boat for two men and may have been used for luggage with smaller, more manoeuvrable, ones being used for passengers. The Hillswick boatmen were probably glad to swap their oars for the kind of motor-driven boat in the picture on the right. Such a launch was also available for tourists to hire for a day out on the water.

In the centre of this view of Hillswick is the hotel built by the shipping company to cater for their package tour passengers. It was a timber construction imported from Norway and erected about 1900. Known originally as the St. Magnus Hotel it has since been restyled St. Magnus Bay Hotel and modified with the addition of modern appurtenances like fire escapes, but it remains substantially as built. To its right, on the edge of the picture, is the impressively large Northmavine Kirk, built in the eighteenth century and modified in the nineteenth. Hillswick House on the shore to the left of the hotel dates from the late eighteenth century, while the wing to its right is thought to be on the site of a seventeenth century trading booth.

This picture taken about 1900 shows the Blade, a sand bar, projecting into Ronas Voe above the settlement of Heylor. Its size has since been reduced causing both Heylor and the shoreline to shrink too. Close to Heylor is a spot known as Hollanders' Knowe where the bodies of Dutch seamen were buried. They died during a battle in 1674 when their ship, a frigate of the Dutch navy, was caught sheltering in the voe by an English frigate.

One of the four Norwegian whaling operations set up at the start of the twentieth century was the Alexandra Whale Fishing Company's station at Collafirth. It is seen here with a whale being cut up on the slipway. The industry carried on for a time after the First World War, but with catches in sharp decline whaling operations off Shetland ceased in the late 1920s. Although their local industry had come to an end many Shetlanders continued to earn their livelihoods up to the 1960s by working at or out of whaling stations on the Falkland Islands and South Georgia.

Ollaberry, on the eastern side of Northmavine, has become a significantly larger township than the one seen in this picture from around the turn of the last century. Even the churchyard, in the foreground, has been has been extended and the ornate carved memorial, seen here projecting above the line of the perimeter wall, now stands alone. The large house in the centre of the picture, Ollaberry Haa, dates from 1789 while the disused United Presbyterian Church on the far side of the bay was erected in 1863.

North Roe is the name given to both the settlement around Burra Voe and the northern part of Northmavine. It is thinly populated as these isolated crofts at Sandvoe (upper) and Setter show. In the foreground of the picture of Setter is a woman performing that most iconic of crofting tasks, milking the cow.

Fethaland, the most northerly point on the mainland, is best known as the location of one of the largest haaf, or deep sea, fishing stations. Such stations were at places often far from the mens' homes, but as close to the fishing grounds as possible. Men, who were obliged to fish for the landowner through the summer months, lived in small booths on the shore and put to sea in small open boats known as sixareens or sixerns, so-called because it took six men to row them. They fished mainly for cod with a baited line and could be at sea for days on end, snatching what sleep they could and sustained only by a little oatmeal. The boats could be operated up to forty miles from land and could be horribly vulnerable if caught in severe weather as occurred in July 1881 when 58 men lost their lives. Other disasters were worse, but this one occurred just five years before the Crofters Holdings Acts of 1886 released men from their ties to the landlords, and a dangerous way of fishing, which they quickly abandoned.

Sunderland and Catalina flying boats were based at Sullom Voe during the Second World War. They carried out anti–submarine and convoy escort duties, but sitting on the water at their base they were vulnerable to enemy air attack and so an airstrip, from which fighter aircraft could protect them, was laid. It became known as R.A.F. Scatsta. These buildings at Graven were erected as part of the base and after the war were turned into the Sullom Voe Hotel. The site overlooked the former wartime base that lay abandoned until the late 1970s when work started on its transformation into the largest oil terminal in Europe. It is a remarkable sight, a massive industrial complex with huge tankers moving in and out, and aircraft taking off and landing at Scatsta airfield, but the hotel is closed.

The R.A.F.'s presence at Sullom Voe attracted so much unwelcome attention from the Luftwaffe early in the war that Sullom can claim to have been hit by one of the first bombs to be dropped on Britain, on 13 November 1939. The incident is recorded in this picture showing a fragment of the bomb being held up for the camera along with the only casualty, a rabbit. The incident gave rise to the popular wartime morale boosting song *Run rabbit, run rabbit, run, run, run!*

Mossbank, seen here in a picture from the early years of the twentieth century, was once the terminal for the ferry to and from Yell before it was moved north to Toft. A more dramatic change occurred during the oil boom of the late 1970s and early 1980s when accommodation for construction workers building the Sullom Voe oil terminal was built along the north side of Firths Voe. A more permanent village has become established since then. At Firth a memorial has been erected to the 22 men from Delting who were lost in a storm while fishing, in December 1900.

Some of the men lost in the Delting fishing disaster came from the crofting community of Swinster. It is seen here looking across the outer of two tombolos that connect the mainland to Fora Ness. The tombolos separate Dales Voe from Swinster Voe where, in common with many sheltered locations, a fish farm has been set up.

The dirt road in the foreground of this picture from the head of Dales Voe has been upgraded to a fast, modern road leading to and from the Yell ferry. The croft house has also been replaced by a more modern structure.

This picture taken from the south side of Firths Voe, before the days of the oil boom, shows only a scatter of houses where the new village has been built. The croft houses in the foreground, on the south side of the voe, are now abandoned and there is certainly no peat stacked outside ready for the onset of winter.

Peat was the crofters' traditional fuel. It was taken from moorland banks where the decaying roots of mosses, heather and other plants built up into a compact mass that could be cut and burned. The top surface of the strip to be worked was cut at the desired distance from the edge of the bank and the turf lifted with a spade and placed where it would re-grow. Then, using a bladed implement called a tushkar, the man (it was usually a man, women often found such work too heavy) sliced slabs of peat from the bank and in the same movement laid them to the side.

The drying process began with the slabs of wet peat being turned regularly for about two or three weeks depending on the weather. The peats were then placed on edge, leaning against each other so that air could circulate around them. As the picture shows this was mostly women's work.

When they were dry enough the peats were taken off the moor. They could be carried by a pony in meshies, nets slung like panniers over a wooden saddle known as a klibber. Ponies were also used to haul peats across the moors in sled-like boxes. People, like the woman on the left, carried peats in a basket known as a kishie and while doing this, women often knitted so that their hands were never idle. Where roads were available the peats were taken to where they could be loaded onto carts. On the right, peats are being taken off high ground by an endless wire arrangement, loaded baskets going down, empty ones coming back up. The last stage of the process was to build the stack, closely packed to withstand wet and windy weather.

To island people the sea is a road, not a barrier, as this advertisement implies. One of the most frequent users of the road between Lerwick and the North Islands was the steamer *Earl of Zetland*, seen here passing Symbister Ness lighthouse. First lit in 1904, the lighthouse was built by the brothers David Alan and Charles Stevenson, the third generation of the famous family of lighthouse engineers.

Fishing was an important part of Whalsay life before the great Shetland herring boom when boats crowded into Symbister Harbour to unload their catches. Sometimes they brought in so many fish that the curing capacity on the shore could not cope and some had to dumped. When the boom ended, fishing faded but was revived during and after the Second World War with boats equipped to catch herring and white fish in season. Norwegian boats scooping up vast quantities of herring in purse seine nets resulted in severe restrictions being imposed from the late 1960s, but the Whalsay fishermen, and the shore-based facilities for handling and processing the catch, have successfully adapted to these and subsequent regulations.

Symbister's modern harbour facilities for fishing boats, ferry and pleasure craft alike are on the west side of the bay, opposite this old harbour and trading booth, or bod, on the east side. Known as Pier House, the booth is a survivor from the days when Hanseatic League merchants from Germany traded a variety of goods for salt fish. Thought to date from the seventeenth century, with nineteenth century alterations, it was restored in 1984 and has subsequently been opened as a museum. The goods hoist, protected by the projecting section of roof, is a fascinating museum piece in itself.

The pier, the end of which is seen on the right of the upper picture, cuts across the foreground here with beyond it, the steamer *Earl of Zetland* standing off on her regular call at Whalsay. The Bruce family, from Unst, took over Whalsay from a number of small local lairds who were not much more than crofter, fishermen themselves. Establishing a subservient, feudal style of rule from their base at Symbister, the family occupied a couple of earlier houses before Robert Bruce built his mansion Symbister House at a cost that came close to impoverishing the family. It became the island's school after the death of the last laird in the 1940s.

Before the advent of ferries the steamer *Earl of Zetland* provided the North Islands with their lifeline. She called at a number of places around South Yell including Burravoe, Gossaburgh and, as here, Ulsta. With no suitable piers the 'Earl' stood off and passengers and cargo were ferried ashore in flit boats, like the one seen here alongside the steamer. The photographer also took the picture of Ulsta Pier. Whoever it was knew they were part of a little bit of history because they captioned the pictures as the *Earl of Zetland's* last trip, but which one? With the ship being brought back into service during the Second World War, she made two last trips, one in 1939 and another in 1946.

The exact date of this picture is also uncertain, although it was used as a postcard on 20 June 1930. The message neatly encapsulates the rhythm of island life: "we are working away, we got our peats turned and most of the sheep rooed, I was at the Arisdale ones on Tuesday." Arisdale runs north through southern Yell from Hamna Voe. The picture is also a snapshot of island life with a farlan and herring barrels on the pier and a man working on his launch in the foreground. Boats, fish, peat and wool is Shetland in a nutshell. With a new pier and ferry terminal, Ulsta has changed significantly although remnants of the old stone pier and the pier house have survived.

The person who took the upper pictures on the facing page also snapped this upturned boat on Yell. They appear to have regarded it as a curiosity although Shetlanders never wasted anything and old boats were often put to use in this way. They were used to house animals although the purpose to which this one was put can only be guessed at. The boat has been raised off the ground to create more headroom inside with the wall below the hull clad in what looks like metal sheeting. The doorway, skylight windows and vents give the structure an air of permanence. The peat stack might be associated with the boat or perhaps with a croft house out of the picture.

Westsandwick is the only settlement of any size on the main road along the west side of Yell. It is seen here looking north along the shore of SouthladieVoe, with the mansion known as North Haa occupying a prominent position at the head of the voe. The oldest part of the house is thought to date from the eighteenth century and to it was added a parallel block in the 1820s along with a showy façade and two flanking pavilions. The overall structure is completed by walled gardens to front and rear.

Yell is almost cut in half by Whale Firth biting deep into the west side and Mid Yell Voe slicing into the east. Mid Yell, on the south side of the voe is the island's main settlement. It is seen in the upper of these two pictures with the old *Earl of Zetland* steamer standing off the small pier and in the lower one with the new *Earl of Zetland* alongside the new pier. Before the new pier was built in 1952 improved road transport within the island had resulted in a reduction in the number of places where the Earl called and these were all stopped after the construction of Mid Yell Pier.

The principal settlement in North Yell is Cullivoe. With its fine natural harbour it was a regular port of call for the *Earl of Zetland* steamer and shared in the great Shetland herring boom. Fishing was revived in the 1930s and received another boost in 1991 when a new pier was built. Cullievoe was also the place from where small boats ferried people to Snarra Voe on Unst before Gutcher was established as the ferry terminal.

Organised ferry services between the mainland and Yell, and across Bluemull Sound between Yell and Unst, started in the 1930s. Buses met the boats at each terminal giving people a real alternative to the *Earl of Zetland* steamer and presenting its operators with some serious competition. The mile-wide Bluemull Sound, with its tidal rip of up to eight knots per hour, was a difficult stretch of water for a small boat, although this one appears to have crossed unscathed with plenty of passengers on board. Vehicular ferries superseded these small boats in 1973, and also rendered the Earl redundant, despite it being the cheapest form of inter island transport.

The island of Fetlar is known as the Garden of Shetland, but it was somewhat deflowered by its nineteenth century owner, Sir Arthur Nicolson. He cleared large numbers of people off the land and, about 1830, built this incongruous looking pile, Brough Lodge, using, if the stories are true, stones taken from sites of antiquity and newly emptied cottages. The island is still feeling the effects of Sir Arthur's attentions, the population is still low and his grand house has lost it bloom.

Laurence Bruce was in a spot of bother in his native Perthshire when his half brother, Robert Stewart, Earl of Orkney and Shetland, encouraged him to escape to Unst. He established a tyrannous regime centred on Muness Castle, the most northerly castle in the British Isles. It was erected in 1598 with circular towers on the north and south corners that convert the rectangular shape of the main structure into a Z-plan layout. The defensive aspect of this arrangement is emphasised by the number and variety of shot holes in the lower walls. Laurence Bruce's son, Andrew, completed the building, but it was abandoned some time later after being sacked and burned by a privateer.

A site close to the Broch of Underhoull was excavated by archaeologists in the early 1960s, revealing the remains of a Viking house that, in common with other such finds, was built on top of an earlier dwelling from the Iron Age. Members of the Unst Field Club assisted on the dig as did volunteers from Aberdeen University and the Royal Air Force. The R.A.F. at Saxa Vord also provided logistical and financial support.

Protected by Uyea Island, Uyeasound has a fine natural harbour that has attracted many of the maritime activities that shaped Shetland over the years. It was used through the sixteenth and seventeenth centuries as a trading centre by Hanseatic League merchants from Germany and it also participated in the herring boom - the pier in this picture, with its rails and bogies, and stacks of barrels in the background, are testimony to that. Fish farms have ensured that the sea and its harvest have continued to be of importance to Uyeasound.

Fish were clearly important to this crofter and his wife (if that's who the well-shod person at the cottage door is). The *Bluebell*, his boat, sits in its noost and all the usual appurtenances for shelling bait, and baiting lines, sit on the bench outside the door. Strings of drying salted fish hang across the front of the cottage and in the background more fish are drying on a line. The pulley block slung from the post on the right indicates a need to tension the line depending on the load.

If there is one aspect of Shetland that is familiar to people throughout the country, perhaps even the world, it is the Shetland Pony. These delightful animals with their short legs, long shaggy mane and tail, and large head in proportion to the body appear from archaeological evidence to have existed on the islands for thousands of years. Random chance and the remoteness of the islands kept those unique characteristics intact until 1890 when the Shetland Pony Stud Book Society was set up to maintain the purity of the breed.

Ponies can be seen everywhere on Shetland, but they are most numerous on Unst. Sales, like the one shown in this picture, have been held annually at Baltasound for some time and from there the ponies can be despatched to new homes around the world. Often the new owners of these friendly little animals are children learning to ride. Events, like the Viking Shetland Pony Show, provide an opportunity for owners to show off their ponies.

They may be cute, but to crofters, ponies were workhorses, employed on the same jobs performed by other breeds of horse elsewhere. One of the main uses they were put to was to work as a pack animal, as shown here, and in that role a major task was to bring peats in from the moor. They also hauled carts, pulled ploughs, and, on the moors, dragged sled-like contraptions loaded with peats. The work could be hard, but at least the air was fresh and the grass sweet by comparison with the tough environment endured by ponies bred to work in coalmines on the British mainland. The picture on the left shows one such pony at a Scottish colliery.

Before the advent of vehicular ferries the only way to get ponies off Unst was by boat. Here a number of animals have been hoisted into the hold of a small boat for a potentially uncomfortable journey to pastures new.

Although many other places were engaged in the great herring boom of the late nineteenth and early twentieth centuries, the level of activity at Baltasound was second to none, with more curing stations in the early years, and at times bigger catches, than Lerwick. During the season hundreds of boats filled the harbour and the local population of 500 was swelled many times over by thousands of itinerant gutters and coopers. At the peak, 1904/05, 250,000 barrels of fish were despatched annually to markets in Eastern Europe and Russia, but as the boom faded the industry gravitated to Lerwick leaving Baltasound with memories and a lot of empty piers.

Some of Baltasound's many piers and gutters' huts can be seen in this picture looking south west to the head of the sound. Fishing, however, is not the area's only industry. Quarries extracting a mineral known as chromite, or chromate of iron, were worked intermittently from its discovery in 1817 to the finding of a larger, better deposit at Hagdale forty years later. Talc has also been worked at Clibberswick, near Haroldswick, since the 1940s and exported through Baltasound.

Unst is the most northerly inhabited island in the British Isles and so almost anything on it has been able to claim to be the most northerly of whatever it is. The Queen's Hotel at Baltasound, for example, used this postcard about 1904 to advertise itself as the most northerly hotel in the three kingdoms and some time later, after a change of name to Hotel Nord, it continued to use the most northerly tag. The smaller Springfield Hotel, in its later guise as the Baltasound Hotel, also (at the time of writing) claims to be Britain's most northerly hotel. There have been some improvements since this picture was taken including the removal of what was presumably the most northerly slightly drunk-looking garden urn.

Within four years of its formation in 1870 to enhance the moral, educational, social and recreational wellbeing of the people of the Mid Parish of Unst, the Unst Working Mens' Society opened the Reading Room at Baltasound. It comprised a small hall with an extension for the library. The caretaker's house was added in the 1890s and in 1908 a new library building was erected. Someone has helpfully marked the date on the appropriate part of the building in this picture and also the date when the new hall was added, 1933 which may also be the date of the picture itself. The Reading Room was extensively redeveloped in the 1980s and remains a popular and attractive public hall.

The most northerly post office in the country has been situated at Baltasound since November 1999 when the office that used to be furthest north, at Haroldswick, closed. Postcards, like this one, provided it with a steady, if small, income. Getting the mail to and from Haroldswick once depended on a courier who travelled south every week, picking up letters at Baltasound and Uyeasound before crossing to Yell from Snarra Voe. More letters were collected at Cullievoe and Mid Yell before they were exchanged for incoming mail at Ulsta. After a night's rest the courier returned north, dropping off mail at all the uplift points. This arduous task came to an end with the advent of regular mail steamers in the 1870s.

Although Unst enjoys a climate moderated by the benign effects of the Gulf Steam, winds can be fierce and the island holds the record for the strongest gust recorded in the British Isles of 177 miles per hour. This picture of Norwick was used by someone to send a message to a friend with these words: "it looks peaceful now, but you should have seen the sea in the south east gale … where the boats are standing, all that was taken away … the small farm is a lot of stones (they) caused a lot of damage, the waves were breaking at the road." The message might refer to January 1937 when Unst experienced the most severe and long-lasting south east gales in living memory.